U0008877

DAILY ORACLE

SEEK ANSWERS
FROM YOUR HIGHER SELF

諭言之書

回答你心中
所有的問題

作──荷莉蔻‧曼迪博 Jerico Mandybur
譯──Adiga

使用方法

看重並愛惜這一本書（還有你的「高我」），每日向它詢問一個深思熟慮後的問題。

一、深呼吸三次，將這本書緊貼近你的心。

二、靜下心來，專注地思考你的問題。在你腦海裡看見這個問題，或是大聲將它說出來。

三、指尖沿著書的所有頁面邊緣撫摸，當你感覺到被呼喚時，停下動作，從停下的地方把書翻開。這就是你的「高我」回應你的答案。

四、相信你讀到的內容，並立刻思考它跟你的問題、你的能量之間的關聯。

遇見「高我」

我們每個人內心深處都有一個「高我」。「高我」是「我們是誰」或「我們來到這個世界之前」的本質。它的存在先於社會制約;在我們決定從宇宙裡獨立出來之前;在我們停止聆聽自己的直覺之前。高我存在於我們擁有恐懼,於我們只知道愛的時候。

你的高我就是你。高我與你所有的意識相互聯繫,並與你同步著,它穿越時空,是一個擁有魔力的你,而且它將永遠存在──比起思想更接近你的靈魂。當你的心在喋喋不休地喊叫時,你的高我卻在細聲細語。這本書是一次安靜的練習──你可以學著傾聽它。

當你向它提出問題後,放慢下來,為自己保留空間,以便讓你的高我進一步給予你答案。記住了,它只為你揭示,但真正掌握答案的人是你──只有在你自己的解釋

裡才能尋獲答案。請相信，你得到的每一個答案，對此時此刻的你來說都是完美的。當你得到答案時，務必知道：你才是自己生命的主宰。

這本書給你的答案有些言簡意賅，有些容易理解，有些則會讓你重新審視自己的問題意識，有些會為你提供足以克服問題的正面幫助。每次引導都是一份授予，從愛出發，從我的高我傳遞到你的高我。它們意圖讓你停下、呼吸並深思，讓神聖的真理走進你的意念與心靈。

親吻並擁抱

荷莉蔻・曼迪博

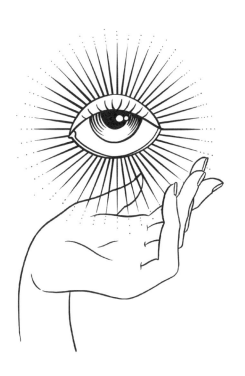

你寧願嘗試後犯錯
還是懊悔每次錯過？

WOULD YOU RATHER MAKE MISTAKES, OR COLLECT REGRETS?

失敗也沒關係
你要勇於嘗試！

THERE'S NOTHING WRONG WITH FAILING.
YOU SHOULD TRY IT!

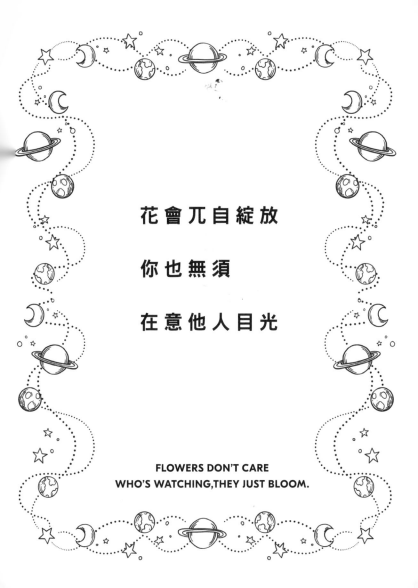

花會兀自綻放

你也無須

在意他人目光

FLOWERS DON'T CARE
WHO'S WATCHING, THEY JUST BLOOM.

揹負既有的包袱
艱辛前進
不如拋卻過往
空著手旅行

YOU CAN'T TAKE YOUR *STUFF* WITH YOU WHEN IT'S OVER.

停止

過度

焦慮

STOP. WORRYING.SO. MUCH.

不要忘記
你是如何走到這裡
才能持續往前挺進

REAL PROGRESS REQUIRES YOU TO RETRACE YOUR STEPS.

機會是源源不絕的

POSSIBILITY IS INFINITELY REPRODUCTIVE.

真實的喜悅
擁有多面向
就像是光
也有陰影

TRUE JOY IS MULTIFACETED;
FULL OF SHADE AS MUCH AS LIGHT.

你值得享有
愈來愈多的平靜

YOU'RE ENTITLED TO ALL OF THE PEACE AND MORE.

是時候了！
向對你無益的一切
說再見

IT'S TIME TO SAY GOODBYE TO WHAT DOESN'T SERVE YOU
ANYMORE.

同理心就是

不要盛氣凌人擺架子

EXERCISING EMPATHY MEANS NOT THROWING
YOUR WEIGHT AROUND.

保持

距離

STAY AWAY.

不快樂的人

總會猛烈攻擊那些

跟自己相似的人

UNHAPPY PEOPLE LASH OUT AT THOSE
THEY SEE THEMSELVES IN MOST.

保護自己
別被負面消極侵擾

SHIELD YOURSELF FROM NEGATIVITY RIGHT NOW.

「質問一切」
即是一種靈修

QUESTIONING EVERYTHING IS A SPIRITUAL ACT.

不要一味向外盲目追求
卻忘記回歸自我的探索

DON'T COUNT ON CERTAIN OUTCOMES INSTEAD OF RELYING
ON YOUR OWN DAMN SELF.

你不是為了每個人而活
你是為了自己而活
為了懂你的人而活

YOU'RE NOT FOR EVERYONE.
YOU'RE FOR YOU, AND THE PEOPLE WHO GET YOU.

雖然現在很辛苦

但是繼續前進吧

一切都是值得的

AS HARD AS IT IS, KEEP GOING.

IT'S WORTH IT.

找一個安靜的地方冥想
你將有意想不到的收穫

FIND A QUIET PLACE TO MEDITATE.
YOU'LL BE AMAZED AT WHAT CAN COME UP.

展現最狂野的自我

LET YOUR MOST WILD,
MESSY SELF EMERGE.

你的指導靈會挺你！

YOUR SPIRIT GUIDES HAVE GOT YOUR BACK.

只在乎別人的想法
你會什麼都得不到

NO ONE EVER GOT ANYWHERE BY GIVING
A F*CK ABOUT WHAT OTHER PEOPLE THINK.

其實沒人知道
自己在幹嘛
不要讓這樣的想法綁住你

NOBODY KNOWS WHAT THEY'RE DOING.
DON'T LET THAT STOP YOU.

靠自己

一點也不孤單

THERE'S NOTHING LONELY ABOUT STANDING ON YOUR OWN
TWO FEET.

所謂「時間」
是由我們建構起來的
也只有我們能
賦予它意義

TIME ONLY HAS THE MEANING AND STRUCTURE WE GIVE IT.

你唯一的任務是

「認識自己」

YOUR ONLY TASK IS TO KNOW THYSELF.

「柔軟」是

「力量」最桀驁不馴的

表達

SOFTNESS IS THE MOST REBELLIOUS EXPRESSION
OF STRENGTH.

等待別人的認同
你將會永遠等待

WAIT FOR PERMISSION,
AND YOU'LL BE WAITING FOREVER.

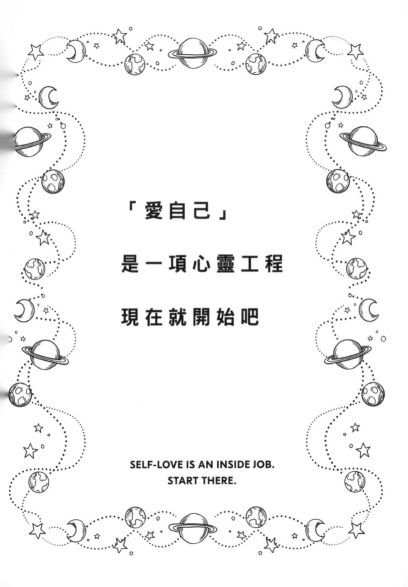

「愛自己」

是一項心靈工程

現在就開始吧

SELF-LOVE IS AN INSIDE JOB.
START THERE.

能敢於夢想
就能勇於實現

IF YOU CAN DREAM IT, YOU CAN MAKE IT HAPPEN.

沒有人是純粹的天使
也沒有人是徹底的惡魔
我們是天使
也是惡魔

NO ONE IS PURE ANGEL OR PURE JERK.
WE'RE ALL BOTH.

採 納 對 你 有 益 的

拋 棄 其 餘 的

HARVEST WHAT SERVES YOU AND LET THE REST GO TO SEED.

集中力量
不要渙散

CONSOLIDATE YOUR POWER INSTEAD OF SPREADING IT THIN.

唯一能治癒你的人
就是你自己
——沒有別人

ONLY YOU CAN EVER HOPE TO HEAL YOURSELF
— NO ONE ELSE.

落實自我

GROUND YOURSELF.

不要被外在環境所定義

REFUSE TO BE DEFINED BY YOUR CIRCUMSTANCES.

你值得擁有
你所渴望的愛
現在
你有對自己示愛的力量

YOU'RE WORTHY OF ALL THE LOVE YOU DESIRE AND
YOU HAVE THE POWER TO SHOW YOURSELF THAT LOVE NOW.

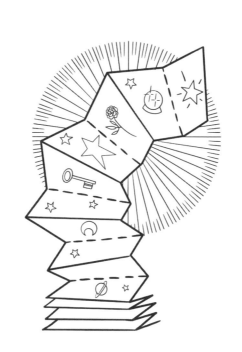

讓事物開展

ALLOW THINGS TO UNFOLD.

除了你自己
沒人能替你的行為
負責

NO ONE IS RESPONSIBLE FOR THE WAY
YOU REACT BUT YOU.

善用你的心

你是自己的

情緒管理員

BE SMART WITH YOUR HEART.
YOU ARE THE STEWARD OF YOUR EMOTIONAL WELL-BEING.

你有創造美好事物的能力
不要浪費它

YOU HAVE THE ABILITY TO CREATE WONDERFUL THINGS.
DON'T WASTE IT.

你是愛的孩子
與一切時空連結

YOU ARE A CHILD OF LOVE, CONNECTED TO ALL SPACE
AND TIME.

生產力

並非

一切

PRODUCTIVITY ISN'T EVERYTHING.

在你擔心其他事之前
先專心守護你的能量

FOCUS ON PROTECTING YOUR ENERGY BEFORE YOU
WORRY ABOUT ANYTHING ELSE.

你要相信
美好的時刻將會來臨

PUT YOUR TRUST IN DIVINE TIMING.

擁抱你的「缺陷」
並愛它們

EMBRACE YOUR 'FLAWS' AND LOVE THEM.

我們不需要理解
高我對我們的計畫
只需要跟隨它

WE DON'T NEED TO COMPREHEND OUR HIGHER POWER'S
PLAN FOR US. WE JUST NEED TO ALLOW IT.

別讓任何人否定你

或是讓你感到卑微

DON'T LET ANY ONE NEG YOU, OR MAKE YOU FEEL SMALL.

所有老掉牙的故事
不再屬於你
開始寫下
屬於你的未來吧

THESE OLD STORIES AREN'T YOURS ANYMORE.
WRITE YOURSELF A NEW FUTURE.

不要再去想那些
不可能發生的事

YOU WOULDN'T BE THINKING IT IF IT WASN'T POSSIBLE.

你沒有被困住

起來

邁步離開

YOU ARE NOT STUCK. GET UP AND WALKAWAY.

不要流連於
囚困住你的
那個內在世界

DON'T STAY SO LONG EXPLORING YOUR INNER WORLD
THAT YOU'RE TRAPPED THERE.

打造堅實不摧的
心靈基石
其餘的部分就會
自己搭建起來

START WITH A STRONG SPIRITUAL FOUNDATION, AND THE
REST WILL BUILD ITSELF.

嘘——

從現在開始

不必擔心

要逃跑或戰鬥了*

SHH, THERE'S NOTHING TO FIGHT OR FLY FROM NOW.

*FIGHT OR FLY，動物面對壓力時，通常會進入戰鬥或逃跑的生理機制。

有時候

我們以為自己想要的

並非自己真正想要的

SOMETIMES WHAT WE WANT TO WANT ISN'T WHAT
WEACTUALLY WANT.

停止空想

開始實踐

STOP DAYDREAMING
AND START DOING .

慢一點！
一心多用意味著
同時做超過一件事
並一事無成

SLOW DOWN! MULTI-TASKING USUALLY MEANS DOING MORE
THAN ONE THING, BADLY.

像對待一個小嬰孩般
培育你自己

NURTURE YOURSELF LIKE A BABY.

現在的你
就是注定要成為的
那個自己

YOU'RE RIGHT WHERE YOU'RE MEANT TO BE.

把腦中的雜音

音量調低

你就能聽到

內在正竊竊私語

TURN THE VOLUME DOWN ON YOUR MIND SO YOU CAN HEAR
YOUR INNER VOICE'S LI'L WHISPER.

你已經可以
邁開步伐奔跑
為何只肯
跨出一小步呢？

WHY TAKE ONE STEP, WHEN YOU COULD START RUNNING?

相信

你的

膽識

TRUST YOUR GUT.

向外探索
你就會尋獲

SEEK AND YE SHALL FIND.

你值得擁有尊嚴
並受到尊重
就像其他人一樣

YOU DESERVE DIGNITY AND RESPECT.
JUST LIKE EVERYONE ELSE.

甩開你的疑惑
擁抱未知的事物

LET GO OF YOUR QUESTIONS. EMBRACE NOT KNOWING.

負面的聲音

並不是真正的你

別把它們當成

你的真實

NEGATIVE THOUGHTS ARE NOT YOU. DON'T MISTAKE THEM
FOR YOUR REALITY.

如果你能意識到
自己多麼強大
結果會如何呢？

WHAT IF YOU REALISED HOW POWERFUL YOU REALLY WERE?

停下來
首先關注
你此時此刻的感受

STOP.
NOTICE HOW YOU'RE FEELING, FIRST.

你身邊其實有人
相當在乎你
看見他們

THERE ARE PEOPLE AROUND YOU WHO CARE A LOT.
SEE THEM.

找一棵樹

然後

用心擁抱它

GO CUDDLE A TREE. SERIOUSLY.

你的經驗

會幫助你

YOUR EXPERIENCE IS VALID.

有些自我感覺良好
並沒有什麼不妥

THERE'S NOTHING WRONG WITH A FEW DELUSIONS OF
GRANDEUR.

絕對不要想一套
做另一套

DON'T EVER LET YOUR CONDUCT BETRAY YOUR CAUSE.

允許自己

簡單活著

GIVE YOURSELF CONSENT TO SIMPLY EXIST.

寶貝
每個人都是
盡其所能

EVERYBODY'S JUST DOING THEIR BEST, BB.

有耐心一點！
緩緩前進並不等於
停滯不前

BE PATIENT.
GOING SLOW DOESN'T MEAN YOU'RE NOT GOING.

你清楚知道
該怎麼做
相信自己

YOU ALREADY KNOW EXACTLY HOW TO BE. TRUST.

你不需要為其他人負責

YOU ANSWER TO NO ONE.

冒牌者症候群*
是一種普遍現象
不要有壓力

IMPOSTOR SYNDROME IS KINDA UNIVERSAL.
DON'T STRESS ABOUT IT.

---

*指一種心理現象。內心浮現懷疑自己的聲音，自認不配、不值得，面對成就卻自我否定，覺得自己僥倖多過實力等。

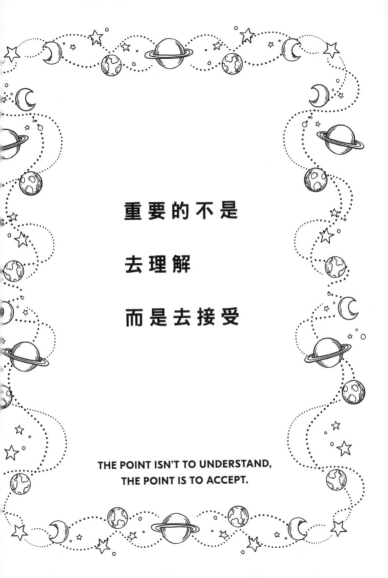

重要的不是

去理解

而是去接受

THE POINT ISN'T TO UNDERSTAND,
THE POINT IS TO ACCEPT.

在做任何事之前
先暫停一下
讓自己復原

TAKE A PAUSE TO RECUPERATE BEFORE YOU DO ANYTHING.

開始其他事情前
先準備好自己

MIND YOUR OWN BUSINESS BEFORE YOU STICK YOUR NECK
INTO OTHER'S.

比起旅行的過程
難道你真的
更在乎抵達目的地？

DO YOU REALLY CARE MORE ABOUT THE DESTINATION THAN
ALL THAT TIME SPENT ON THE JOURNEY?

往好的一面看
肯定你所擁有的

SEE THE GOOD. ACKNOWLEDGE WHAT YOU HAVE.

「別人比較好」是個狡猾的騙徒

COMPARISON IS A TRICKY BITCH.

你並不是
別人嘴裡說的
那個你

YOU ARE NOT WHAT THEY SAY YOU ARE.

該斷不斷

必受其亂

LET GO, OR BE DRAGGED.

心之所在
家之所處

‘HOME’ IS WHEREVER THE HELL YOU WANT IT TO BE.

這個世界並非
一片小小的派
它大到足夠
分給每個人享用

THE UNIVERSE IS NOT A PIE. THERE'S MORE THAN ENOUGH TO
GO AROUND.

每件事物
都被引導
只為了
抵達這一刻

EVERYTHING HAS BEEN LEADING UP TO THIS MOMENT.

第 一 步 ：

不 要 庸 人 自 擾

STEP ONE IS UNPACKING THAT QUESTION YOURSELF.

你正在接受測試
採取切實的行動
並謹守你的信念

YOU'RE BEING TESTED.
STEP UP AND HONOUR YOUR TRUTH.

你的感性
就是你的超能力

YOUR SENSITIVITY IS YOUR SUPERPOWER.

在對的時間點
一次只做一件事

ONE THING AT A TIME AND EACH WHEN IT'S TIME.

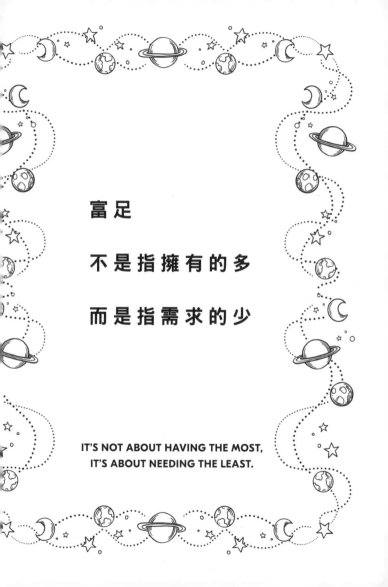

富足

不是指擁有的多

而是指需求的少

**IT'S NOT ABOUT HAVING THE MOST,
IT'S ABOUT NEEDING THE LEAST.**

「自愛」

意味著

先照料你的

最基本需求

SELF-CARE MEANS TENDING TO YOUR MOST BASIC NEEDS
FIRST.

像愛別人那樣愛自己
為何就這麼難？

WHY IS IT SO HARD TO SHOW YOURSELF THE LOVE YOU
SHOW OTHERS?

你會感到驚訝的

YOU'D BE SURPRISED.

停下來
你所期待的解答
會在寂靜之中
被尋獲

STOP. THE ANSWERS YOU'RE CRAVING ARE FOUND IN
STILLNESS.

你是備受呵護的

YOU ARE PROTECTED.

付出多少
就會
得到多少

YOU'LL GET OUT EXACTLY WHAT YOU PUT IN.

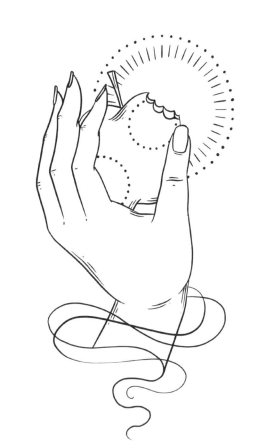

不要才剛播種
馬上就想收成

DON'T EXPECT TO EAT THE FRUIT IF YOU'VE ONLY JUST
PLANTED THE SEED.

鬆開你的手

LOOSEN YOUR GRIP.

結果不是重點

THE OUTCOME IS NOT THE POINT.

你值得
擁有更多

YOU ARE WORTHY OF MUCH MORE.

向你的內心探詢
當對的時機來臨時
你才知道該怎麼做

SEARCH YOUR HEART.
YOU'LL KNOW WHAT TO DO WHEN THE TIME COMES.

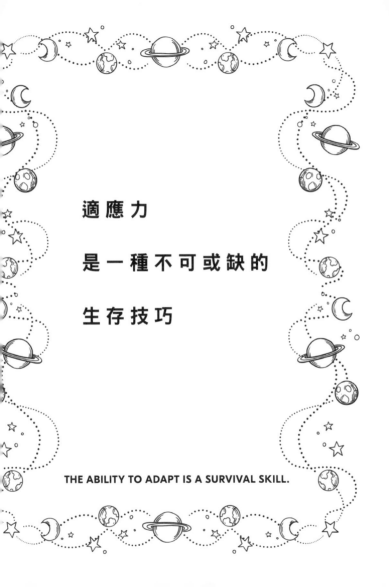

適應力

是一種不可或缺的

生存技巧

THE ABILITY TO ADAPT IS A SURVIVAL SKILL.

把你調整成
知道自己值得的狀態

ALIGN YOURSELF TO WHAT YOUR SPIRIT ALREADY KNOWS
YOU DESERVE.

別犯傻

還不是結束的時候

DON'T BE FOOLED. THIS ISN'T WHERE IT ENDS.

無論面臨什麼情況
都該用愛終結恐懼

IN EVERY INSTANCE, CHOOSE LOVE OVER FEAR.

放

下

它

LET. IT. GO.

這就是你一直在
等待的預示

THIS IS THE SIGN YOU'VE BEEN WAITING FOR.

你說「好」
整個宇宙
也會這樣回應你

SAY 'YES' AND THE UNIVERSE WILL ECHO IT BACK TO YOU.

該開始努力了

IT'S TIME TO GET TO WORK.

精通「耐心」

這項技能

你絕對不會後悔

PATIENCE IS A SKILL YOU'LL NEVER REGRET MASTERING.

不要被你的自尊心控制
多傾聽你的靈魂

YOUR EGO IS NOT IN CHARGE, YOUR SPIRIT IS. LISTEN TO
THAT INSTEAD.

別再看輕自己

STOP PLAYING SMALL.

事實不會都跟
表象一樣

NOT EVERYTHING IS WHAT IT SEEMS.

知道得愈多
懷疑得愈多

GOETHE WAS ON TO SOMETHING WHEN HE SAID 'DOUBT
ONLY GROWS WITH KNOWLEDGE'.

面對生命的奧祕
深感自我的卑微
這種心態
跟榮耀是沾不上邊的

THERE'S NO HONOUR LIKE BEING HUMBLED BEFORE THE
MYSTERIES OF LIFE.

如果你從來不疑惑

早已知道一切答案

你就不能有所成長

IF YOU KNEW THE ANSWER, THERE WOULD BE NO LESSON.

別再助長
你的負面思維

DON'T FEED THE TROLLS IN YOUR HEAD.

過去讓它過去

THE PAST IS IN THE PAST.

你比你想像的
還要強大

YOU'RE STRONGER THAN YOU REALISE.

沒錯

ABSOLUTELY.

一直關注
假想的「缺陷」
只不過是一種
精神自虐

FOCUSING ON YOUR SUPPOSED 'DEFECTS' IS A FORM OF
EMOTIONAL SELF-ABUSE.

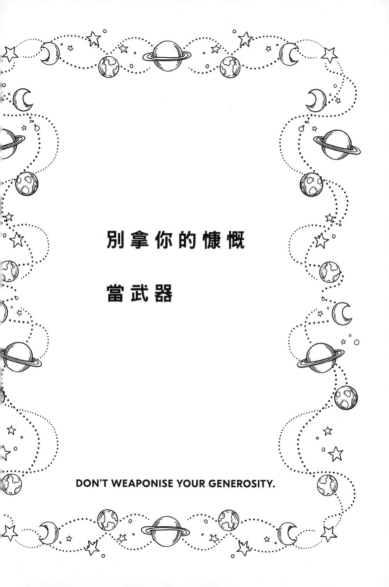

別拿你的慷慨

當武器

DON'T WEAPONISE YOUR GENEROSITY.

如果大家都從
一座橋上往下跳
你也會跟著跳嗎？

IF EVERYONE ELSE JUMPED OFF A BRIDGE, WOULD YOU DO IT?

沒有挫敗
無法成長

WITHOUT FAILURE, WE WOULD NEVER LEARN.

優雅地向前挺進

MOVE FORWARD WITH GRACE.

如果無法寬恕他人
至少記得原諒自己

IF YOU CAN'T FORGIVE THEM, AT LEAST FORGIVE YOURSELF.

透過他人觀點
來認識自我
是具啟發性的

SEEING YOURSELF THROUGH SOMEONE ELSE'S EYES IS
ILLUMINATING.

「自愛」
是讓所有其他的愛
得以紛紛湧現的
一口噴泉

SELF-LOVE IS THE FOUNTAIN FROM WHICH ALL OTHER LOVES
SPRING.

靜靜地坐

細細傾聽

SIT STILL, AND LISTEN.

有想實現的目標
難道就得一直有門路？

WHAT IF THE STUFF YOU WANT TO MANIFEST, YOU HAD
ACCESS TO ALL ALONG?

深呼吸

感覺腹部鼓脹

保持憋氣

數到三

慢慢吐出氣

重複

BREATHE IN DEEPLY THROUGH YOUR NOSE, FEELING YOUR
BELLY EXPAND. HOLD FOR THREE COUNTS. EXHALE FULLY
THROUGH YOUR MOUTH. REPEAT.

一切都會好起來

EVERYTHING IS GOING TO BE JUST FINE.

真正的自由就是不要
被結果牽著鼻子走

TRUE FREEDOM IS NOT BEING ATTACHED TO THE OUTCOME.

不要樂觀得太早

DON'T COUNT YOUR CHICKENS, CHICKEN.

一直回頭無法讓你
往前邁進

LOOKING BACK SO OFTEN WON'T PROPEL YOU FORWARD.

「短缺」
是一種既有結構
它會迫使我們去
掠奪其他人

'LACK' IS A CONSTRUCT THAT WOULD SEE US DEPRIVE
OTHERS.

你無法替換
自己的生命
但你也不會因此
失去什麼

NOTHING IS MISSING FROM YOUR LIFE THAT YOU CAN'T
REPLACE YOURSELF.

別把事情看得太重
親愛的　放輕鬆

IT'S NOT THAT SERIOUS, HONEY. RELAX.

持續相信

DON'T STOP BELIEVING.

只有那些

你願意做的事

你才有可能

把它們做好

YOU CAN ONLY DO SOMETHING WELL IF YOU'RE WILLING TO
DO IT POORLY FIRST.

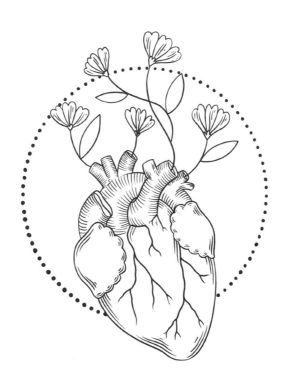

暫時擱置你的腦子
聽聽你的心怎麼說？

IGNORE YOUR HEAD FOR A SECOND. WHAT DOES YOUR
HEART SAY?

你可以

（也應該）

做得更好

YOU CAN (AND SHOULD) DO BETTER.

別想那麼多
讓自己感受

STOP THINKING SO MUCH, AND LET YOURSELF FEEL.

謹 慎 對 待

你 的 情 緒

自 我 克 制

BE CAREFUL WITH YOUR EMOTIONS. USE TEMPERANCE.

徹底誠懇
始終如一

TELL THE WHOLE TRUTH, ALWAYS.

不要見樹不見林

DON'T IGNORE THE BIGGER PICTURE.

換位思考
就是你需要克服的功課

WHAT YOU CAN'T STAND IN OTHERS IS AN UNRESOLVED PART
OF YOU.

「生活」是一座螺旋梯

你會一次一次重複遭遇

每一次都要比上一次進步

LIFE IS A SPIRAL STAIRCASE. YOU WILL CONFRONT THIS
AGAIN AND AGAIN, WISER EACH TIME.

要更懂得策略性思考
不要一味地全力以赴

BE STRATEGIC, NOT ALL-OUT SNEAKY.

你的祖先
正在看顧著你

YOUR ANCESTORS ARE WATCHING OVER YOU.

想像充滿了
「如果當初⋯⋯」
這種懊悔的人生
把握當下好好去做吧

IMAGINE A LIFE FULL OF 'WHAT IFS'. NOW, DO THE THING.

與其尋找機會
不如創造機會

IF YOU'RE LOOKING FOR OPPORTUNITIES, CREATE THEM.

你不會再理會
虛妄詭詐之人

DECEITFUL PEOPLE DON'T GET YOUR ATTENTION ANYMORE.

「信念」是一盞
永不熄滅的燈

CONVICTION IS A LIGHT THAT CAN NEVER BE BLOWN OUT.

你是唯一可以

對自己喊停的人

YOU ARE THE ONLY PERSON WHO CAN REALLY STOP YOU.

認清事實
你腦海中的喧囂
對你沒有好處

THE NOISE IN YOUR HEAD ISN'T HELPING ANYMORE.
SEE IT FOR WHAT IT IS.

不要畫蛇添足

DON'T GILD THE LILY.

何不來一場

你最喜歡的精神革命
....

**WHAT WOULD [INSERT YOUR FAV SPIRITUAL
REVOLUTIONARY] DO?**

鬆開你的觀點
以免讓它窒息

HOLD YOUR VISION TOO TIGHTLY AND YOU RISK
SMOTHERING IT.

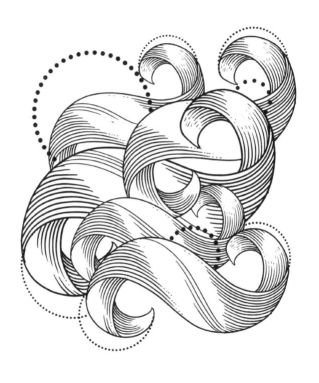

保 持 平 衡 ——

「 強 度 」 可 以 任 你

歡 欣 鼓 舞 地 驅 策

也 可 能 摧 毀 你

INTENSITY IS A WAVE YOU CAN RIDE, ELATED — OR IT CAN
WIPE YOU OUT. USE BALANCE.

不必尋求他人
你就是解答

DON'T SEEK IN OTHERS WHAT YOU CAN FIND IN YOURSELF.

一切值得的事情

都不容易

NOTHING WORTHWHILE IS EASY.

若今天的感覺不對
明天還是不會變好

IF IT DOESN'T FEEL RIGHT TODAY, IT WON'T FEEL RIGHT
TOMORROW.

每揭去一層幻象
愈可以看見真實

IF YOU WANT THE TRUTH, SIMPLY STRIP AWAY EVERY
ILLUSION.

別管別人

專注自己

STAY IN YOUR OWN LANE.

不要改變你的夢想

改變實現它們的方式

DON'T CHANGE YOUR DREAMS, CHANGE THE WAY YOU'RE
GOING TO REACH THEM.

最好的關係
是和能讓我們更深切
認識自我的人為伴

THE BEST RELATIONSHIPS ARE WITH PEOPLE THAT TEACH US
MORE ABOUT OURSELVES.

大事降臨的時候
會怎麼發展
完全取決於你的
行動

SOMETHING BIG IS COMING. YOUR ACTIONS WILL HELP
DETERMINE WHAT IT IS.

雖是老生常談
但這才是正解——
跟著你的感覺走

IT'S A CLICHÉ BECAUSE IT'S TRUE – YOU NEED TO FOLLOW
YOUR HEART.

如果不好好檢查
你的傷口
你又如何能
好好清理？

IF YOU DON'T EXAMINE YOUR WOUNDS, HOW CAN YOU
EXPECT TO CLEAN THEM?

小心輕放
把自己當作
一件寶物

BE GENTLE. YOU'RE PRECIOUS CARGO.

先 停 止 心 裡 的 風 暴

等 到 能 真 正 傾 聽 時

向 你 的 心 再 提 問 一 遍

SETTLE THE STORMS IN YOUR MIND, THEN ASK AGAIN WHEN
YOU'RE REALLY LISTENING.

學著

當一塊海綿

BE A SPONGE. LEARN.

掌握你的力量

你是強大的

你可以自己做主

STAND IN YOUR POWER.

YOU ARE STRONG.

YOU ARE SOVEREIGN.

無論如何
都要捍衛自己的權益

FOR BETTER OR WORSE, THE SQUEAKY WHEEL GETS THE
GREASE.

確認你的故事

只屬於你

然後你可以開始書寫它

ACKNOWLEDGE YOUR STORY AS YOUR OWN, SO YOU CAN
START WRITING IT FOR YOURSELF.

淨化你自己
與你的空間

CLEANSE YOURSELF AND YOUR SPACE.

沒有人虧欠你

那麼

你虧欠自己了嗎？

NOBODY OWES YOU ANYTHING. SO WHAT DO YOU OWE YOURSELF?

我們都有陰暗面
審視自己的陰暗面
你將受益匪淺

EVERYONE HAS A SHADOW SELF. BE WILLING TO PEEK AT
YOURS, AND YOU'LL LEARN A LOT.

你可以是自己

最嚴厲的批評者

或是自己最慈善的朋友

端看你怎麼選擇

YOU CAN BE YOUR HARSHEST CRITIC, OR YOUR OWN BEST
FRIEND. CHOOSE.

船到橋頭自然直

YOU'LL CROSS THAT BRIDGE WHEN YOU COME TO IT.

當你被自己的意識

打了一巴掌

你醒了

PAIN IS BEING SLAPPED IN THE FACE BY CONSCIOUSNESS.
YOU'RE AWAKE.

所有跡象顯示：

「是」

ALL SIGNS POINT TO 'YES'.

展現自信
才能展現自我的價值

SHOW UP FOR YOURSELF, SO YOU CAN SHOW UP FOR
OTHERS.

試著搞懂
你的「不明白」
它並不像火箭科學
那樣晦澀難懂

IF YOU 'DON'T KNOW', JUST COMMIT TO FIGURING IT OUT. IT'S NOT ROCKET SCIENCE.

別去理會那些
想要證明「你是誰」
的人

DON'T LISTEN TO PEOPLE WHO EXPLAIN WHO YOU ARE.

即興一下又何妨

IT'S OKAY TO IMPROVISE.

不要再傻坐枯等

你可以

推動世界的改變

**DON'T JUST SIT THERE.
BE AN AGENT OF CHANGE IN THE WORLD.**

只要是人
就會面對這種事

IF YOU WEREN'T DEALING WITH THIS, YOU WOULDN'T BE
HUMAN.

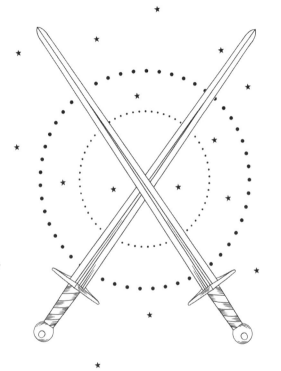

你有捍衛自己的權力

YOU HAVE EVERY RIGHT TO STAND UP FOR YOURSELF.

懂得愈多

需要愈少

THE MORE YOU KNOW, THE LESS YOU NEED.

你不需要
把每件事都想明白

YOU DON'T NEED TO HAVE EVERYTHING FIGURED OUT ALL
THE TIME.

意志是你
最強而有力的工具
你要對使用它的方式
負起責任

YOUR WILL IS YOUR MOST POWERFUL TOOL. BE RESPONSIBLE
WITH HOW YOU WIELD IT.

對你無益的人事物
只會拖累你

WHAT DOESN'T SERVE YOU IS SLOWING YOU DOWN.

有時候這並不是
你的問題

SOMETIMES, IT'S NOT ABOUT YOU.

宇宙說──「你很棒」

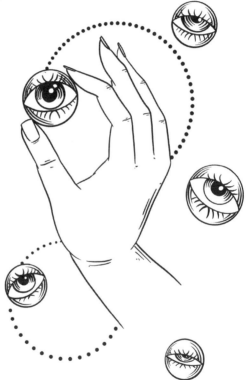

不要在乎別人的眼光

CAN YOU SEE YOURSELF THROUGH THEIR EYES?

「懷疑」

是一種靈性實踐

TO DOUBT IS A SPIRITUAL ACT.

你可以從虛無之中
創造出事物

YOU CAN MAKE SOMETHING OUT OF NOTHING.

打開心扉

OPEN THE F*CK UP.

三思而後行

LOOK BEFORE YOU LEAP.

當我們接受測試時
也是展示真實的時刻

WHEN WE'RE TESTED IS WHEN WE REVEAL OUR TRUEST
SELVES.

「自信」
是開啟動機的
鑰匙

SELF-BELIEF IS THE KEY TO ANY FORM OF MOTIVATION.

如果感覺左右為難
讓自己掙脫出來

WHEN YOU'RE CAUGHT BETWEEN A ROCK AND A HARD
PLACE, JUST WIGGLE OUT.

人們正在告訴你

他們的真實面貌

傾心聆聽

PEOPLE ARE CONSTANTLY TELLING YOU WHO THEY REALLY
ARE. PAY ATTENTION.

那些你會幫好友擋掉的
也該替自己擋一擋

IF YOU WOULDN'T WANT IT FOR YOUR BEST FRIEND,
DON'T ACCEPT IT FOR YOURSELF.

那些徹底榨乾你的人事物
無權如此

WHAT DRAINS YOU IRREDEEMABLY HAS NO BUSINESS HERE.

我們都是過來人

EVERY BODY FEELS THIS WAY.

「明天」是一個
完美藉口
就跟減肥一樣

'TOMORROW' IS THE PERFECT EXCUSE BECAUSE IT NEVER
COMES.

心靈隸屬於個人
而隸屬個人的一切
都是政治性的

THE SPIRITUAL IS PERSONAL AND THE PERSONAL IS
POLITICAL.

「高我」即是你

THE HIGHER POWER IS YOU.

生命意義

由你賦予

THE MEANING OF LIFE IS WHAT EVER YOU BRING TO IT.

看見世界的美好事物
並全心接受

SEE THE GOOD IN THE WORLD, AND RECEIVE IT.

假如你不誠懇
即便得到鑽石
也會化為灰燼

GETTING WHAT YOU WANT MEANS NOTHING IF YOU GAVE
AWAY YOUR INTEGRITY.

如果只有石頭
試著點石成金

ALCHEMISE WHAT'S IN FRONT OF YOU INTO SOMETHING
ELSE.

半途而廢的投入
只會得到半途而廢的結果

HALF-ARSED EFFORTS YIELD HALF-ARSED RESULTS.

發光發亮

無須羞愧

THERE'S NO SHAME IN SHINING.

當你可以綜覽全局
就別為了枝微末節而懊惱

DON'T SWEAT THE MINOR DETAILS WHEN THERE'S A BIG
PICTURE TO ABSORB.

不必尋求肯定
也別跟現狀低頭

STOP LOOKING FOR VALIDATION
AND SURRENDER TO WHAT IS.

你是被愛的

YOU ARE LOVED.

生活就是一所學校

應該時時保持虛心求教

LIFE IS A SCHOOL. DON'T BE ONE OF THOSE KIDS WHO
THINKS THEY ALREADY KNOW EVERYTHING.

為你的心保有空間

HOLD SPACE FOR YOUR HEART.

傷逝很正常

邁步向前也是

MOURNING THE PAST IS NATURAL.
SO IS MOVING ON.

親愛的
遲到總比不到好

BETTER LATE THAN NEVER, SWEETIE.

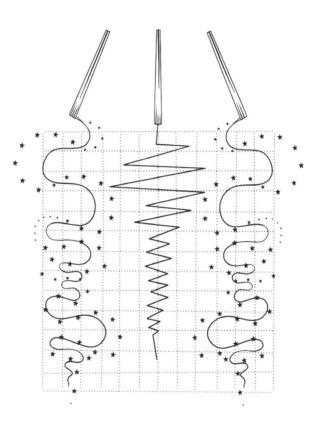

啟動你的
「鬼扯探測器」
好好看清
事實的真相

FIRE UP THE BULLSH*T DETECTOR
AND SEE THINGS FOR WHAT THEY ARE.

你擁有深度挖掘
需要的所有工具

YOU HAVE EVERYTHING IT TAKES TO DIG DEEP.

「正常」
不過是烘衣機上的
一種功能設定

'NORMAL' IS A SETTING ON THE DRYER.

接 受 你 所 得 到 的 一 切

BE RECEPTIVE TO WHAT'S BEING OFFERED TO YOU.

故作軟弱是一回事
你應該更加真實

FAUX-VULNERABILITY IS A THING. MAKE YOURS REAL.

適可而止

EVERYTHING IN MODERATION.

汽車保險桿貼紙
說的對——
奇蹟真的會發生

THE BUMPER STICKERS WERE RIGHT: MAGIC DOES HAPPEN.

每個人背後都有故事
分享你的故事
也傾聽別人的

EVERYONE HAS A STORY. SHARE YOURS AND LISTEN TO
THEIRS.

別人的不安全感
與你無關

THEIR INSECURITIES ARE NOT YOUR REALITY.

過去只有一個你
本來也只有一個你
你是唯一的

THERE HAS ONLY EVER BEEN, AND WILL ONLY EVER BE,
ONE YOU.

你還沒準備好知道

YOU'RE NOT READY TO KNOW.

天下沒有白吃的午餐

THERE'S NO SUCH THING AS A FREE LUNCH.

全心全意地忠於自己

你永遠不會感到孤單

COMMIT TO YOURSELF WHOLEHEARTEDLY AND YOU'LL
NEVER BE LONELY.

快樂是會蔓延的
找到它　然後分享它

YOUR JOY IS CONTAGIOUS. FIND IT AND SHARE IT.

生活就是一種挑戰
好好把握

LIFE ITSELF IS A CHALLENGE. RISE TO IT.

慢慢來

LITTLE BY LITTLE.

你靈魂裡的東西
須透過你來發光

WHAT'S IN YOUR SOUL HAS A RIGHT TO SHINE THROUGH
YOU.

不要光看外表就下判斷
的確是這樣

IT'S TRUE WHAT THEY SAY ABOUT NOT JUDGING
A BOOK BY ITS COVER .

你能喊停
你知道你可以的

YOU CAN STOP. YOU KNOW YOU CAN.

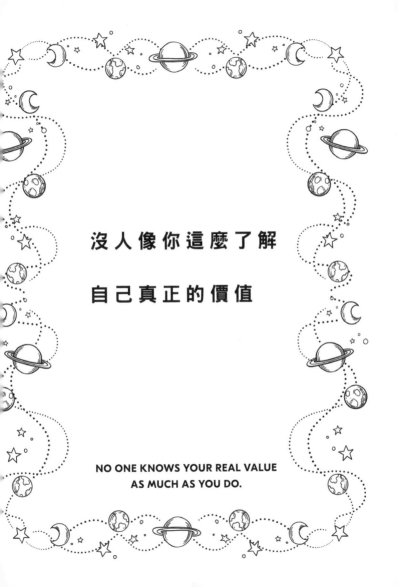

沒人像你這麼了解

自己真正的價值

NO ONE KNOWS YOUR REAL VALUE
AS MUCH AS YOU DO.

正義一定會伸張

JUSTICE WILL BE SERVED.

「成功」不過是個
無人企及的抽象字眼

'SUCCESS' IS JUST AN ABSTRACT WORD THAT NO ONE EVER
RELATES TO.

好好思考
你想得到什麼

THINK ABOUT WHAT YOU THINK YOU WANT VERY
CAREFULLY.

我並不是用來占卜的

神奇八號球*

請更嚴肅思考問題

專注

然後再次提問

I'M NOT AN EIGHT BALL. TAKE YOUR QUESTION MORE
SERIOUSLY, FOCUS, AND ASK AGAIN.

---

*也譯作魔力八球，是一種占卜用的道具。

別為不重要的事憂愁
轉移注意力
去做更重要的事

STOP SWEATING THE THINGS THAT DON'T MATTER AND PAY
ATTENTION TO THE ONES THAT DO.

「紀律」
是創造與成長
不可或缺的要素

DISCIPLINE IS AN ESSENTIAL PART OF CREATIVITY AND
GROWTH.

比你想的更接近

IT'S CLOSER THAN YOU THINK.

把自己擺在第一位

PUT YOURSELF FIRST.

即使很多事物
眼睛看不到
也不要否認
它們存在的事實

THERE ARE A LOT OF THINGS WE CAN'T SEE.
DOESN'T MAKE THEM LESS TRUE.

一旦你清楚有多少人

抱持著荒謬的見解

你就會了解大眾流行時尚

其實毫無意義

WHEN YOU SEE HOW MANY PEOPLE HOLD SH*TTY OPINIONS,
YOU REALISE POPULARITY MEANS NOTHING.

展現

SHOW UP.

你無法挑著
千斤萬擔趕路
還期待自己能夠
看清前途
放下吧

YOU CAN'T SEE IN FRONT OF YOU WHEN YOU'RE CARRYING
SUCH A LARGE BURDEN AROUND. DROP IT.

誰會在乎這需要
耗費多少時間？

WHO CARES HOW LONG IT TAKES?

你的價值
不是你的產量
所能衡量的

YOU ARE SO MUCH MORE THAN YOUR OUTPUT.

我們共享著
一樣的目標：
愛與被愛

WE ALL SHARE THE SAME PURPOSE; TO LOVE AND TO BE
LOVED.

有時候
你需要的就只是休息

SOMETIMES THERE'S NOTHING YOU NEED TO DO BUT REST.

現在和未來

都沒有理由退縮

**THERE'S NO REASON TO BE HOLDING BACK,
NOW OR EVER.**

我們不能用物質
衡量一個人

MATERIAL THINGS ARE NOT THE MEASURE OF A PERSON.

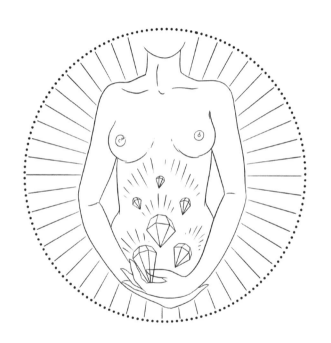

我們逃避的那部分
就是掩埋
珍貴寶藏的地方

THE PARTS OF OURSELVES WE AVOID ARE WHERE THE GEMS
LIE.

如果你會失去某物
那麼它一開始就不是
真的屬於你

WAS IT EVER TRULY YOURS TO BEGIN WITH?

不是每個人都了解

你的價值

所以你怎麼做很重要

NOT EVERYONE WILL UNDERSTAND YOUR WORTH, THAT'S
WHY IT'S CRUCIAL YOU DO.

心存感恩

GRATITUDE IS EVERYTHING.

說「妨礙不了我」
然後持續前進

SAY 'NOT TODAY SATAN' AND MOVE ON.

親愛的
別害怕面對
已經在你眼前發生的事

DON'T BE AFRAID TO OPEN YOUR EYES TO WHAT'S ALREADY
IN FRONT OF YOU, LOVE.

你若逃避了自己
必須解決的問題
生活自有一套
「鏡像反饋系統」
會再次把這些問題
帶回你的眼前

LIFE HAS A WAY OF MIRRORING BACK TO YOU WHAT NEEDS
ADDRESSING.

輕而易舉得到

也會輕而易舉失去

EASY COME , EASY GO.

這就是付出一切後
最好的結果嗎？

IS IT IN THE BEST INTERESTS OF ALL INVOLVED?

設立邊界
然後只讓最好的事物進入

SET FIRMER BOUNDARIES. LET ONLY THE BEST THINGS PASS THROUGH.

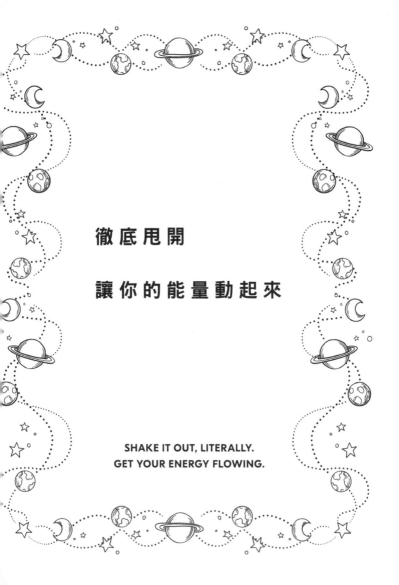

徹底甩開

讓你的能量動起來

SHAKE IT OUT, LITERALLY.
GET YOUR ENERGY FLOWING.

如果你什麼都不做
請別指望會有任何
好事發生

DON'T EXPECT ANYTHING WITHOUT DOING ANYTHING.

「返璞歸真」

是清理大腦最快的方法

你該這樣做

GETTING INTO NATURE IS THE QUICKEST WAY TO CLEAR
YOUR HEAD. AND YOU SHOULD.

罪惡感
是一種無法回饋自我的
無用情緒

GUILT IS A USELESS EMOTION WITH ZERO REDEEMING
QUALITIES.

你是變形大師
你能改造自己

YOU ARE A SHAPESHIFTER. ALLOW YOURSELF TO
TRANSFORM.

無論問題多麼讓人怯步

只要好好溝通就能解決

HOWEVER DAUNTING THE QUESTION, COMMUNICATION IS
ALWAYS THE ANSWER.

你的熱情
會把你帶往
想去的任何地方

YOUR PASSION WILL GET YOU EVERYWHERE.

簡單的事情

不配稱為「工作」

THEY DON'T CALL IT 'DOING THE WORK' BECAUSE IT'S EASY.

跟你身邊的人
互相合作
別互相對抗

WORK WITH – NOT AGAINST – THE PEOPLE AROUND YOU
NOW.

看見你想追求的
然後確認你能
逐一將它們實現

VISUALISE WHAT YOU WANT, AND THEN MAKE SURE IT
COMES TRUE.

沒有徹底體驗
就無法真正了解

YOU WON'T UNDERSTAND UNTIL YOU FULLY EXPERIENCE.

愛惜你所擁有的

好好看重它們

CHERISH WHAT'S YOURS AND RESPECT THEIRS.

「善良」
有時需要擁有
說「不」的能力

KINDNESS SOMETIMES MEANS SAYING 'NO'.

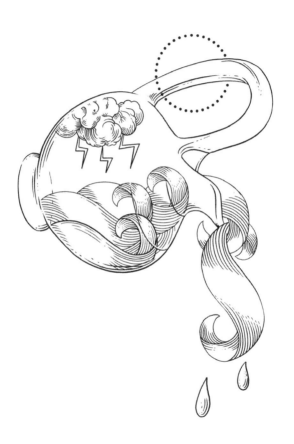

憤怒是對的
但要淺嘗則止
讓它刺激一下就好

YOUR ANGER IS RIGHTEOUS. TAKE A SIP AND LET IT FUEL
YOU, BUT DON'T GUZZLE ITS POISON.

為何疲於奔命呢？

思考一下吧

WHY SO HASTY? THINK ABOUT IT.

無常的定律

將會是一種折磨

WHEN YOU'RE OVERLY ATTACHED TO HOW THINGS ARE, THE
CONSTANT NATURE OF CHANGE IS TORTURE.

這是事實
還是聽說？

IS THAT THE TRUTH, OR JUST A STORY YOU HEARD?

你的「直覺」
是一份很棒的禮物
善用它

YOUR INTUITION IS THE GREATEST GIFT YOU HAVE. USE IT.

沒有人可以看見
你的感受
外人只能夠看見
你的行為

NO ONE CAN SEE WHAT YOU'RE FEELING. THEY CAN ONLY
SEE YOUR ACTIONS.

無須聽天由命

THERE'S NO NEED TO LEAVE ANYTHING TO CHANCE.

阿不然你想怎樣

IT IS WHAT IT IS.

不要忽略

深度連結的需求

你需要找人聊一聊

DON'T NEGLECT YOUR NEED FOR DEEP CONNECTIONS. YOU
ARE A SOCIAL BEING.

做自己需要勇氣
但會很快樂

IT TAKES BRAVERY TO BE AUTHENTIC. BE THAT GUY.

如果對方要求你

喬裝扮演

而非無條件

接納真正的你

其實你不必忍受

YOU DON'T HAVE TO TOLERATE BEING ASKED TO PERFORM
INSTEAD OF JUST BEING ACCEPTED AS YOU ARE.

每個念頭都像
一句咒語
你必須挑揀適合的使用

EVERY THOUGHT IS A SPELL.
CAST THE RIGHT ONES.

你的潛力無窮無盡

YOUR POTENTIAL IS ENDLESS.

事實證明

沒有人知道所有的答案

差得遠了

SURRENDER TO THE FACT THAT NO ONE HAS ALL THE
ANSWERS. NOT EVEN CLOSE.

不斷祝福

BLESSINGS ON BLESSINGS.

減輕情緒負擔
就能透徹看清

LIGHTEN YOUR EMOTIONAL LOAD AND YOU'LL SEE THINGS
MORE CLEARLY.

從別人的

期望枷鎖中掙脫

解放自己

RELEASE YOURSELF
FROM THE SHACKLES OF THEIR EXPECTATIONS.

你的身體是一座寺廟
請用面對聖物般
虔敬的心善待它

YOUR BODY IS A TEMPLE.
TREAT IT LIKE THE SACRED THING IT IS.

「富足」
是一種心理狀態

ABUNDANCE IS A STATE OF MIND.

我的回覆是

「不」

MY SOURCES SAY NO.

你無法改變過去

但你能改變看待它的方式

YOU CAN'T TAKE BACK WHAT'S COME TO PASS BUT YOU CAN
CHANGE HOW YOU THINK ABOUT IT.

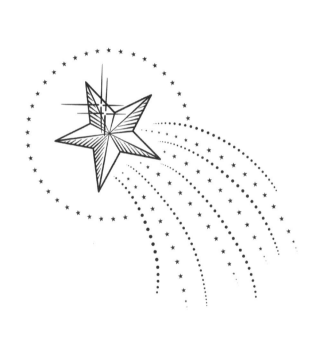

或許你還未找到
你的人生座標
但你知道它一定存在

YOU DON'T EVER SEE YOUR NORTH STAR, YOU JUST TRUST
YOU HAVE ONE.

你的想像力是
所有知識與意義的來源
相信它

YOUR IMAGINATION IS A LEGITIMATE SOURCE OF
KNOWLEDGE AND MEANING. BELIEVE.

「給予」是前往
「獲得」的捷徑

THE QUICKEST WAY TO BE SERVED IS TO BE OF SERVICE.

時候到了

你可以的！

NOW IS THE TIME. YOU CAN DO IT!

抱歉
世界並不是
繞著你轉

YOU'RE NOT THE CENTRE OF EVERYTHING. SORRY.

害怕也沒關係
但你真的不用害怕

IT'S OKAY IF YOU'RE SCARED, BUT YOU DEFINITELY DON'T
NEED TO BE.

你有需要誓死捍衛嗎？*

IS THIS REALLY A HILL YOU'RE WILLING TO DIE ON?

---

*hill to die on為軍事用語，原意是指不計代價也要占領的高地要塞，衍伸為某事非常重要，不論多困難、付出任何代價都要攻克它。

投身所愛

不求回報

DO WHAT YOU LOVE, EVEN IF YOU NEVER GET PAID FOR IT.

你永遠無法以火滅火

有些事情

只需放手

任由燃燒殆盡

YOU CAN'T ALWAYS FIGHT FIRE WITH FIRE. WITH SOME, YOU HAVE TO JUST LET THEM BURN OUT.

除了你自己
沒有人可以擁有你
或使你完整

NOBODY OWNS OR COMPLETES YOU, BUT YOU.

冬眠也沒有關係
你將會脫胎換骨

IT'S OKAY TO HIBERNATE. YOU'LL COME OUT STRONGER.

「掌控」是一種幻覺

沒有什麼是

我們真正能掌控的

而且這樣

也沒有什麼不好

'CONTROL' IS AN ILLUSION. NOTHING IS UNDER CONTROL
AND THAT'S FINE.

提防假先知*

BEWARE OF FALSE PROPHETS.

---

*語出《聖經 馬太福音》7:15：「你們要提防假先知。他們披著羊皮來到你們當中，骨子裡卻是凶殘的狼。」（Beware of false prophets, who come to you in sheep's clothing, but inwardly are ravening wolves.）

羞愧不屬於你

你只是接受了

放下它吧

YOUR SHAME IS NOT YOURS, YOU'VE JUST TAKEN IT ON. LET
IT GO NOW.

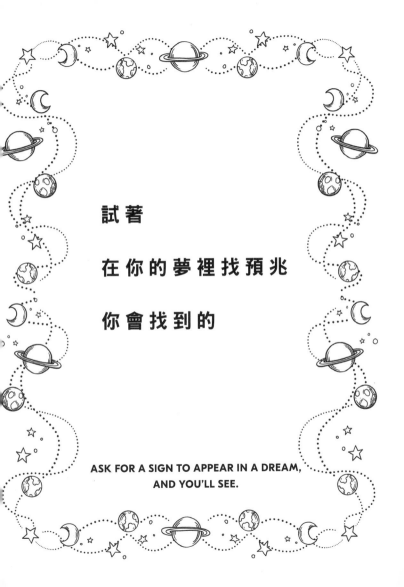

試著

在你的夢裡找預兆

你會找到的

ASK FOR A SIGN TO APPEAR IN A DREAM,
AND YOU'LL SEE.

展現自己
找到舞台

LET YOURSELF BE SEEN. TAKE UP SPACE.

事情總是來得很快
該把自己準備好

THINGS ARE GOING TO HAPPEN, AND FAST. BE READY.

別為了不曾擁有的事物
費心傷神
該好好想想你所擁有的

IT'S WHAT YOU HAVE (NOT WHAT YOU DON'T HAVE)
THAT'S WORTH THINKING ABOUT.

是 時 候 了

好 好 駕 馭

邏 輯 與 理 性 的 力 量

**NOW IS THE TIME TO HARNESS ALL THE POWERS OF YOUR
LOGIC AND RATIONALITY.**

盡力去做
明智以對

GO FOR IT! JUST BE SMART ABOUT IT.

你的內心小孩
正對你說：
「我愛你 我以你為榮
一切都沒問題的」

'I LOVE YOU SO MUCH AND I'M PROUD OF YOU. IT'S OKAY.' —
YOUR INNER CHILD

沒有人可以壟斷真相

NOBODY HAS A MONOPOLY ON THE TRUTH.

活著
要接受真正的
自己

LOOK IN THE MIRROR. FULLY ACCEPT YOURSELF. GO LIVE LIKE
IT.

讓你心中的神

也能認可別人的神

LET THE GOD(ESS) IN YOU ACKNOWLEDGE THE GOD(ESS)
IN THEM.

改變思考的角度
你會看得更透徹

CHANGE YOUR PERSPECTIVE AND YOU'LL SEE THINGS MORE
CLEARLY.

這是一場
你能勝利的戰鬥
確認一切
公平行事

THIS IS A BATTLE YOU CAN WIN,
SO MAKE SURE YOU'RE PLAYING FAIR.

你將展翅重生

（沒錯，

你就是隻浴火鳳凰）

YOU'LL RISE AGAIN (YEP, LIKE A PHOENIX).

沒 有 什 麼 會 真 的 消 亡

它 們 只 是 發 生 了 轉 變

NOTHING REALLY DIES, IT'S JUST TRANSMUTED.

「保持謙卑」是
「自豪」的反面
你需要兩者兼備

STAYING HUMBLE IS THE FLIP SIDE OF BEING PROUD. YOU
NEED BOTH.

你還能擁有更多

THERE IS MUCH MORE OUT THERE FOR YOU.

你可以抵禦
最猛烈的暴風雨

YOU CAN WITHSTAND THE MOST INTENSE OF STORMS.

不想跟別人
追求一樣的事物
又有何妨

IT'S OKAY TO NOT WANT THE SAME THINGS AS EVERYBODY
ELSE.

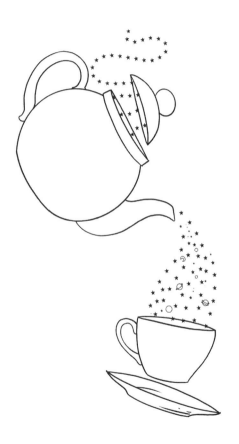

在平凡裡找到詩意
你將更加享受自己

FIND THE POETRY IN THE MUNDANE AND YOU'LL ENJOY
YOURSELF A LOT MORE.

寶貝

你當之無愧

YOU EARNED IT, BABE.

其實你已經知道答案
撥出時間把它弄明白

YOU ALREADY KNOW THE ANSWER.
TAKE TIME AWAY TO FIGURE IT OUT.

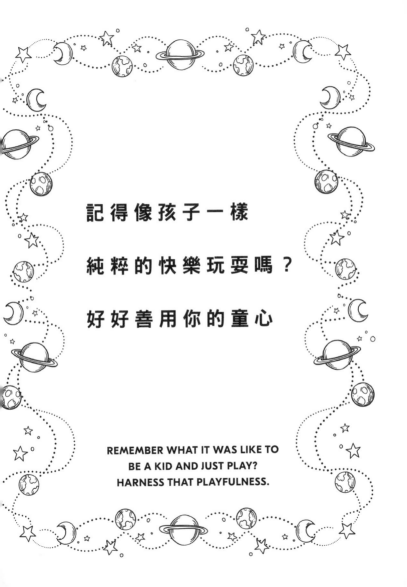

記得像孩子一樣

純粹的快樂玩耍嗎？

好好善用你的童心

REMEMBER WHAT IT WAS LIKE TO
BE A KID AND JUST PLAY?
HARNESS THAT PLAYFULNESS.

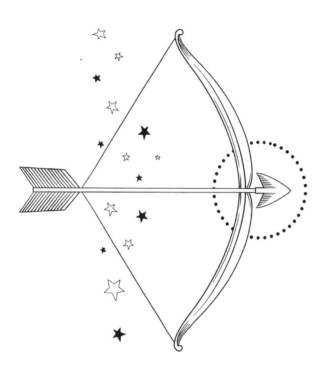

成為一名勇士
兌現你的力量

EMBODY THE WARRIOR. STEP INTO YOUR POWER.

「煩惱」會讓你誤以為

它最重要

DISTRACTIONS HAVE A WAY OF MAKING THEMSELVES LOOK
LIKE THE MOST IMPORTANT THING.

你會渡過這次難關
更難、更糟的處境
你都經歷過了

YOU CAN GET THROUGH THIS.
YOU'VE GONE THROUGH WORSE.

即 使 想 法 極 佳

觀 點 教 人 信 服

仍 有 許 多 不 足

等 待 你 的 學 習

YOUR IDEAS ARE AMAZING AND YOUR OPINIONS VALID.
DOESN'T MEAN YOU DON'T HAVE A LOT STILL TO LEARN.

如果有東西摔碎了
或許這是一個機會
讓你用更好的方式
將它們拼湊回來

WHEN THINGS FALL APART, IT'S A CHANCE TO PUT THEM
BACK TOGETHER IN A BETTER WAY.

沒有什麼會一直存在

沒有

NOTHING IS PERMANENT. NOTHING.

蒐集更多資訊
以便讓你形塑
自己的見解

SEEK OUT MORE INFORMATION SO YOU CAN FORM YOUR
OWN OPINION.

慷慨地施
慷慨地受

RECEIVE AS GENEROUSLY AS YOU GIVE.

好的關係
可以讓你變得赤裸
並將你帶回
真我之中

THE BEST RELATIONSHIP WILL EXPOSE YOU AND BRING YOU
BACK TO YOURSELF.

你最黑暗的部分
正在呼喚著
被愛
被接受

THE DARKEST PARTS OF YOURSELF ARE CRYING OUT FOR
LOVE AND ACCEPTANCE.

保持低調
別惹麻煩

KEEP YOUR HEAD DOWN AND STAY OUT OF TROUBLE.

讓該來的來
讓該走的走

LET WHAT COMES, COME. LET WHAT GOES, GO.

靈 感 就 像 肌 肉

它 需 要 投 入 鍛 鍊

通 過 練 習 舉 起

你 的 心 靈

INSPIRATION IS LIKE A MUSCLE. IT TAKES DEDICATION AND
PRACTICE TO LIFT YOUR SPIRITS.

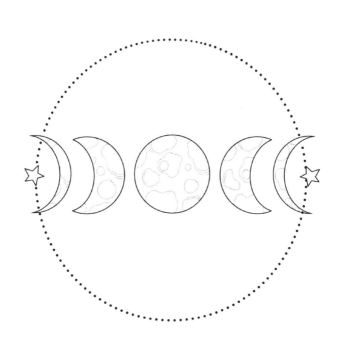

結束
代表下一個開始

THE END IS ALWAYS JUST THE BEGINNING AGAIN.

寶貝

保持緩慢與平穩

SLOW AND STEADY, BABY.

我們無法迴避因果

THERE'S NO ESCAPING THE LAWS OF KARMA.

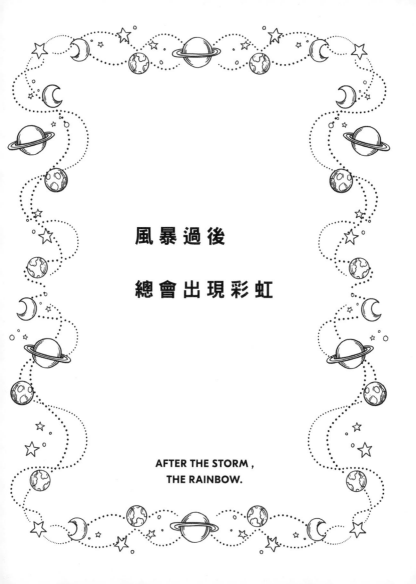

風暴過後

總會出現彩虹

AFTER THE STORM ,
THE RAINBOW.

ACKNOWLEDGEMENTS:

Thank you to my higher self and Spirit for guiding me in writing this book. Thank you to Kajal, Bex, Claire, and everyone at Hardie Grant and Chronicle Books for your hand in bringing this to life. Thank you to Jenny MY Dubet for your incredible eye.

Thank you to the teachers, facilitators, and healers (both human and non) who've helped get to me this point.

Deep thanks to my friends and family for the support, patience, and love.

And thank you to my Scorpio love, Ariel Katz — the answer to all my questions.

致謝詞：

感謝我的高我，感謝聖靈引領我撰寫了這本書，也感謝卡潔兒、貝克斯、克萊兒和哈迪‧葛蘭，以及記事報出版每一位幫忙接生這本書的同仁。感謝慧眼獨具的「我的」珍妮‧杜貝。感謝在我完成它的過程裡為我提供了教導、協調與療癒的對象（無論是人或物）。深深銘感我的親友給予的支持、耐心與愛。並感謝我的天蠍座愛人艾瑞爾‧凱茲──你是我所有問題的答案。

諭言之書　回答你心中所有的問題

作者	荷莉蔻・曼迪博（Jerico Mandybur）
譯者	Adiga
責任編輯	陳思安
特約編輯	Adiga
美術設計	La Vie編輯部
行銷企劃	謝宜瑾

發行人	何飛鵬
事業群總經理	李淑霞
副社長	林佳育
主編	葉承享
出版	城邦文化事業股份有限公司 麥浩斯出版
E-mail	cs@myhomelife.com.tw
地址	104台北市中山區民生東路二段141號6樓
電話	02-2500-7578
發行	英屬蓋曼群島商家庭傳媒股份有限公司城邦分公司
地址	104台北市中山區民生東路二段141號6樓
讀者服務專線	0800-020-299（09:30～12:00; 13:30～17:00）
讀者服務傳真	02-2517-0999
讀者服務信箱	Email: csc@cite.com.tw
劃撥帳號	1983-3516
劃撥戶名	英屬蓋曼群島商家庭傳媒股份有限公司城邦分公司
香港發行	城邦（香港）出版集團有限公司
地址	香港灣仔駱克道193號東超商業中心1樓
電話	852-2508-6231
傳真	852-2578-9337
馬新發行	城邦（馬新）出版集團Cite（M）Sdn. Bhd.
地址	41, Jalan Radin Anum, Bandar Baru Sri Petaling, 57000 Kuala Lumpur, Malaysia.
電話	603-90578822
傳真	603-90576622

總經銷	聯合發行股份有限公司
電話	02-29178022
傳真	02-29156275

製版印刷	凱林彩印股份有限公司
定價	新台幣450元／港幣150元

2024年2月初版 4 刷・Printed In Taiwan
版權所有・翻印必究（缺頁或破損請寄回更換）
ISBN　978-986-408-666-5 [精裝] 978-986-408-681-8 [ePub]

國家圖書館出版品預行編目［CIP］資料

諭言之書：回答你心中所有的問題／荷莉蔻・曼迪博
［Jerico Mandybur］著；Adiga翻譯. -- 初版. -- 臺北市：
城邦文化事業股份有限公司麥浩斯出版：英屬蓋曼群
島商家庭傳媒股份有限公司城邦分公司發行, 2021.05
　面；　公分
譯自：Daily oracle : seek answers from your higher self.
ISBN 978-986-408-666-5 [精裝]

1.格言

192.8　　　　　　　　　　　　110004655

Daily Oracle
Copyright © 2019 HARDIE GRANT BOOKS, AN IMPRINT OF HARDIE GRANT UK LTD.
 'First published in the United Kingdom by Hardie Grant Books in 2019'
This Complex Chinese characters edition is published in 2021 by My House Publication, a
division of Cité Publishing Ltd.
Through The PaiSha Agency.
All rights reserved.